Christopher Wren and St. Paul's Cathedral

Ronald Gray

Published in cooperation with Cambridge University Press
Lerner Publications Company, Minneapolis

Editors' Note: In preparing this edition of *The Cambridge Topic Books* for publication, the editors have made only a few minor changes in the original material. In some isolated cases, British spelling and usage were altered in order to avoid possible confusion for our readers. Whenever necessary, information was added to clarify references to people, places, and events in British history. An index was also provided in each volume.

LIBRARY OF CONGRESS CATALOGING IN PUBLICATION DATA

Gray, Ronald D.
    Christopher Wren and St. Paul's Cathedral.

    (A Cambridge topic book)
    Includes index.
    Summary: An account of the construction of St. Paul's Cathedral in London by Christopher Wren after old St. Paul's was destroyed by fire in 1666. Also discusses other Wren churches and buildings and the relation of Wren's style to his historical period.
    1. Wren, Christopher, Sir, 1632-1723. 2. St. Paul's Cathedral (London, England) [1. Wren, Christopher, Sir, 1632-1723. 2. St. Paul's Cathedral (London, England)] I. Title.
    NA997.W8G65 1982   726′.6′0924   81-13696
    ISBN 0-8225-1222-X (lib. bdg.)   AACR2

This edition first published 1982 by Lerner Publications Company by permission of Cambridge University Press.

Original edition copyright © 1979 by Cambridge University Press as part of *The Cambridge Introduction to the History of Mankind: Topic Book.*

International Standard Book Number: 0-8225-1222-X
Library of Congress Catalog Card Number: 81-13696

Manufactured in the United States of America

This edition is available exclusively from:
Lerner Publications Company, 241 First Avenue North, Minneapolis, Minnesota 55401

1 2 3 4 5 6 7 8 9 10 86 85 84 83 82

Contents

1 Gothic and Renaissance *p.4*
Circle or cross? *p.4*
The language of classical architecture *p.6*
Classical architecture comes to England *p.8*

2 Young Wren *p.9*
Boy and young man *p.9*
The Sheldonian Theatre, Oxford *p.11*
College buildings in Cambridge *p.12*

3 After the Great Fire *p.16*
The Fire of 1666 *p.16*
A plan for the City *p.17*
The City churches *p.19*

4 Planning the cathedral *p.25*
A circular church? *p.25*
The Warrant design *p.27*

5 Building the cathedral *p.28*
Demolition *p.28*
Stone for St Paul's *p.28*
Preparations on the site *p.30*
Building the nave *p.31*
Difficulties *p.34*
Building continues *p.35*
Decorations *p.40*

6 Architecture: a new profession *p.43*
The architecture of the new Caesars *p.43*
Wren eclipsed *p.45*

Glossary of Architectural Names
   And Terms p. 49
Index p. 50
Acknowledgments p. 51

The bust of Wren made by Sir Edmund Pierce in 1673, now in the Ashmolean Museum, Oxford.

1 Gothic and Renaissance

Circle or cross?

The shape of a building can make a difference to your feelings. Long narrow corridors can feel stifling; broad well-lit halls give a sense of freedom. Sometimes the shape also has a meaning which needs explanation. A large number of the churches and cathedrals built in the Middle Ages are shaped like a cross. Many people have interpreted this shape as symbolising the body of Christ, crucified on the cross (though the builders may have had no such idea in mind).

Many of the churches of the Middle Ages were in a style which we now call Gothic. They had tall pointed windows, and pointed arches inside. The windows were full of richly coloured stained glass, and the whole interior was painted in glowing colours. The longer part of the cross, called the nave, was separated from the shorter part (the chancel) by a screen. Unless you were a priest or choirboy you could seldom go beyond this, except to see the relics of some saint or to pray at his shrine. The two 'arms' of the cross were known as the transepts. On either side of the nave there were lower parts called aisles (*aile* is French for 'wing'). A high-roofed nave with two lower aisles was typical of Gothic cathedrals as well as of Norman ones, which preceded them.

Soon after the year 1400 – about the time of Henry V and Joan of Arc – churches began to be thought of in a new way. This was connected with a much more general change which is called the Renaissance, meaning rebirth. For many years

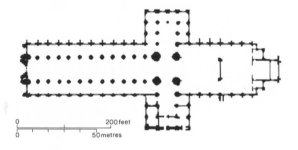

0 — 200 feet
0 — 50 metres

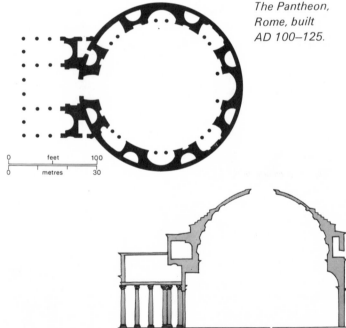

The Pantheon, Rome, built AD 100–125.

0 — feet — 100
0 — metres — 30

above: *The shape of a cross can be seen very clearly in the ground plan of Winchester Cathedral. It is the longest Gothic church in Britain, and measures 170 metres (556 ft) from east to west.*

right: *Cross-section of a typical medieval cathedral.*

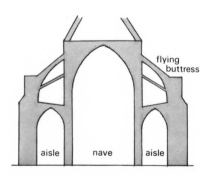

flying buttress

aisle   nave   aisle

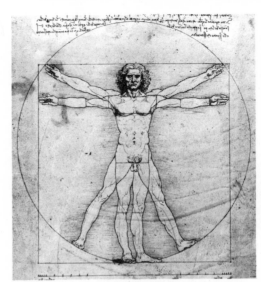

Leonardo da Vinci made this drawing to show how the proportions of a human figure could be fitted into a circle (the symbol of eternity and God's perfection) or into a square, another shape regarded by Renaissance architects as perfect.

before 1400 some artists and scholars, especially in Italy, had thought of the times of ancient Rome as a great period in the history of civilisation which they would like to renew. Rome had been and still was an Italian city, and some Italians felt that what Italians had done once they could do again. They began now to dig up Roman sculptures, and study the ruins of Rome which you can still see. Some of the architects were interested in the round-shaped, ancient temple called the Pantheon, which also still survives in Rome, though it is now used as a church.

At the same time they began to think more about the shape that a church might have. From the earliest times, some Christian churches had been circular. For instance, the churches which the Knights Templar had built in the Middle Ages were based on a circular plan like the Holy Sepulchre in Jerusalem. Some Roman and Greek philosophers had also written about the special quality of circles, which were to them a symbol of God himself. These men believed that everything in the universe had a mathematical and harmonic structure. The most perfect geometrical figure they could think of was the circle. The human body could be fitted into such a figure, symbolising that Man was made in the image of God.

Some Renaissance architects believed that if churches were circular, they could express the perfection of God. One architect, rather given to exaggeration, even said that prayer would not be properly effective if the church was not built with the correct proportions. But most of the architects who built round churches between 1490 and 1530 did not go in for theory; they were practical men, not philosophers. All the same, when the Pope required a new design to replace the old cathedral of St Peter in Rome, the architect Bramante immediately thought of a round shape. It seemed the most holy expression of the perfection, omnipotence, truth and goodness of God. At the same time, Bramante made his design look rather like the Pantheon.

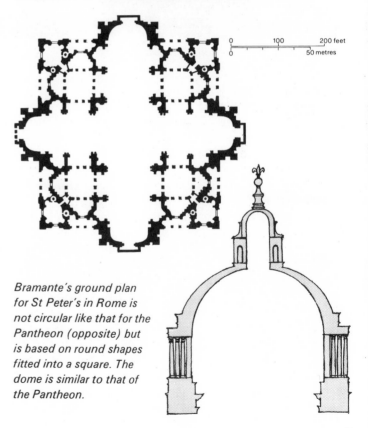

Bramante's ground plan for St Peter's in Rome is not circular like that for the Pantheon (opposite) but is based on round shapes fitted into a square. The dome is similar to that of the Pantheon.

above: *The Colosseum in Rome, built AD 73–80.*

right: *These drawings, from a book by Claude Perrault published in 1676, show five different styles (called orders) of Roman columns. Left to right: Tuscan, Doric, Ionic, Corinthian, Composite.*

The language of classical architecture

When Roman architecture began to be deliberately imitated, Roman books were also studied – although they had never been totally neglected. The only surviving Roman book on architecture was one by Vitruvius who described certain details closely and explained them. You can see some of the details in this picture of the Colosseum, the building in ancient Rome where huge audiences watched while gladiators fought and wild beasts were hunted or paraded. Looking closely, you see that at each storey there are pilasters (pillars set against a wall) and, looking closer still, you can just see that at each storey the tops (or capitals) of the pilasters are slightly different. On the bottom storey they are quite plain, on the one above they look as though they are rolled round in a whorl, and on the next above that they are feathery, like a plant. The shape of these pilasters, columns and capitals came to be very important in the Renaissance. Architects felt that by imitating closely what the Romans had done they might rival them or even do better.

As a result, from the fifteenth century onwards, many buildings were decorated with the three 'orders' found on the Colosseum: the Doric, the Ionic and the Corinthian; and preferably in the same sequence, with the Doric at the bottom and the Corinthian at the top. Not to follow this sequence was like making a mistake in grammar. Sometimes the orders were used with Vitruvius's explanations in mind. He said the Doric order showed 'the proportion, grace and strength of a man's body', the Ionic showed 'feminine slenderness', and the Corinthian imitated 'the slight figure of a girl'. (As often happens architecture was being thought of in terms of a human body.) There were two other Roman orders which do not appear on the Colosseum, the Tuscan and the Composite.

The space between the columns also mattered to the Romans. Slim columns far apart feel free and stately – if they

above: *A drawing of Palazzo Çaprini in Rome, designed by the architect Bramante in 1512, and later lived in by the painter Raphael. It was demolished in the seventeenth century.*

right: *A triumphal arch built in Rome in AD 82 by the Roman Emperor Titus.*

below right: *The church of S. Andrea at Mantua in Italy begun in 1470. Compare the arches along each side of the nave with the photograph of the Arch of Titus above.*

are not too far apart for their width – while thick columns close together can feel powerful. Columns or pilasters in pairs make a different impression, and if they are raised on an upper storey, as they were in Bramante's Palazzo Caprini, they look down majestically. Notice too the massive, rough-looking stones on the ground floor, which give a feeling of crude power. This treatment of stones is called rustication, and 'rustic', meaning countrified, suggests something rough. The building designed by Bramante has a noble lightness resting on very strong foundations. The noblemen for whom such palaces were made probably thought of themselves like that.

Sometimes the shapes of Roman buildings were used for Christian churches. The design of the fourth-century church of St Mary Major in Rome is based on the basilicas, or meeting halls, which stood in the forums of Roman towns. Similarly, the architect Alberti built a church in Mantua in 1470 which has a row of great triumphal arches forming the two sides of the

below: *S. Francesco della Vigna in Venice: Palladio's idea for a classical façade to cover up the Gothic church behind it.*

right: *The Banqueting House in Whitehall. Built in 1619, the squared, box-like shape, as well as the rows of columns along the outside were unlike anything most Englishmen had ever seen before.*

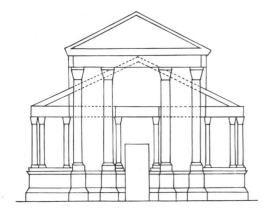

nave, imitating the arches set up by the Roman emperors to commemorate their victories.

Another great Italian architect, Palladio, designed all his buildings with a close attention to geometrical proportions. It may be that he even thought of his buildings, in a way, as expressing through mathematics a kind of heavenly music. He probably believed that the proportions of a beautiful building should be like the proportions of the vibrations of a string producing different notes of music. He thought that such a relationship was typical of the divine quality of the arts. But if we look at one of Palladio's earliest works, we can see how he tried to convert an already existing Gothic building into a Renaissance one. There was in Venice a Gothic church with a high nave and two low aisles, rather like the one shown on page 4. Palladio was asked to make the front (or façade) of this look like a Roman temple. It was a difficult task, since Roman temples, unlike Roman basilicas, did not have lower aisles at the sides. His solution was to make a kind of double temple, the main one covering the end of the nave, and the other one showing only at the sides, in front of the aisles. We can imagine the two roofs at the sides joining together exactly in the middle of the main temple, as in the drawing. This was

a neat and harmonious way of fitting the new to the old, even though the view of the façade from behind shows that it does not exactly correspond to the shape of the old church. The façade is really a mask.

Classical architecture comes to England

The man who did most to introduce the 'Italian' style to England was Inigo Jones, who worked during the reigns of James I and Charles I. Jones was a great admirer of Palladio, and, though many of his buildings have disappeared, you can still see his clear, radiant work at the Queen's House, Greenwich, and at the Banqueting House opposite the Horse Guards in Whitehall. Inside, it is wonderfully bright and calm. For Englishmen of his day it was revolutionary. In Shakespeare's time Whitehall Palace was not very much more than a village of Tudor timbered houses, alleys, wharves, without any overall design. Jones's Banqueting House stood high above it all, and not only in actual height: it is a noble, serene building, such as England had never seen before. Not many years after it was completed, however, England was plunged into civil war.

2 Young Wren

Boy and young man

The civil war, which lasted on and off from 1640 to 1651, was basically a conflict between Parliamentarians and Royalists. The Parliamentarians believed that the king, Charles I, had misused his power by refusing to cooperate with Parliament in governing the country. Those on the Royalist side supported the king as the absolute ruler of England.

The struggle also had a religious character since many of the Parliamentarians were advocates of the extreme form of Protestantism known as Puritanism, while the Royalists were generally connected with that part of the English church most like the Roman Catholic church. These two different religious groups had very different attitudes towards art and architecture. Puritans believed in simplicity and austerity, and many of them despised the decorative arts. 'High Church' Royalists, on the other hand, usually approved of luxuries like the Whitehall Banqueting House, especially when they were beautiful and fashionable.

The military struggle between the two sides ended in victory for the Parliamentarians, and in 1649, Charles I was executed on a platform erected in front of the Whitehall Banqueting House. The Puritan leader Oliver Cromwell assumed power, but by 1660, Cromwell was dead, and Charles II, the son of the dead king, had been restored to the throne. Charles was sympathetic to Catholicism and very much in favor of luxurious living. Large-scale building, which had almost stopped during the war, began again with vigor during the 1660s.

At about this time, a young man named Christopher Wren was beginning to make a name for himself. He had been born in 1632, at East Knoyle in Wiltshire, where his father was rector of the parish church. His family was Royalist; his

Part of a map of London, drawn by Visscher in 1620, showing Southwark Cathedral in the foreground, London Bridge and the spires of many of the old churches of the City.

The Royal Observatory, Greenwich, which you can still visit. Wren designed this building for observing the skies. After the restoration of the monarchy in 1660, Charles II – his portrait is on the wall – and many other leading men encouraged scientific studies, and it was then that the Royal Society was founded.

father became Dean of Windsor before Christopher was two, and so was very close to the royal family, and his uncle, the Bishop of Ely, was imprisoned by the Parliamentarians in the Tower for eighteen years. When Christopher was still only ten, the great Civil War of 1642–6 in England began and Parliamentary soldiers pillaged his father's Deanery. But from all these experiences of harsh struggle he seems to have kept only the wish to be at peace with everybody. All his life he had many friends, and few enemies.

As a boy Wren soon became interested in astronomy. He had a gift for making things with his hands. He liked to see his ideas or theories turned into real objects. In his early years he made a model showing the relation of the earth, the sun and the moon. He also designed a clockwork machine for recording wind and rainfall. More of his curious inventions included a device for writing in the dark and a pen for writing in duplicate. Another instance of his liking for making ideas into solid objects was his model showing how muscles work.

From school at Westminster, Wren went to Wadham College, Oxford, where he took his BA in 1651. He was becoming a brilliant mathematician, and astronomy took

more and more of his time, though he also gave attention to things like a transparent beehive, a statue which seemed to speak, a model of the human eye, and an enormous magnet. Soon he got to know the famous scientist Robert Boyle, and performed an important experiment on a dog to prove to him that poison could be carried by the bloodstream to the heart. He was very experienced, in fact, in anatomical dissection. But it was still astronomy which he preferred, and after some years of research on the planet Saturn he was appointed Professor of Astronomy at Gresham College, London, in 1657.

All this may not sound like a good preparation for a career as an architect. Wren was lucky, of course, to belong to a prosperous, educated family, and after 1660 royal favour helped him. In those days the older type of builder, the master-mason who was the 'Hed, the Provost, the Director, and Judge' of all building works and builders (as John Dee wrote in 1570), was giving way to a new kind of man, the gifted amateur. It was part of the Renaissance ideal that a man should be able to turn his hand to anything, like the Italian, Leonardo da Vinci, who was a painter and also invented aeroplanes and tanks, planned cities with traffic-canals and designed fortresses and excavators. Wren, in any case, was good at most things he undertook; he was just that kind of man. So when in 1660 he sent some drawings of insects as they appeared under a microscope (a new invention then) to Charles II, the king was instantly impressed by his talent. He asked Wren to make a model of the moon and, when he supplied that, the king's next request was that he should design fortifications for a British naval base at Tangier. Men of genius were expected to switch easily from one thing to another, and though Wren turned down the request to go to Tangier – or rather, in the language you used to the king in those days, 'humbly prayed His Majesty to command his duty in England' – he was a success at Court, which counted for a great deal.

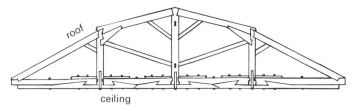

roof

ceiling

right: *The ground plan of the Theatre of Marcellus in Rome, built in 11 BC.*

below: *The Sheldonian Theatre. The early nineteenth-century view of the interior shows the painted ceiling. The exterior view was published in 1675.*

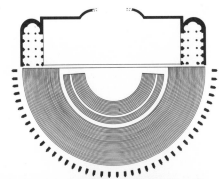

The Sheldonian Theatre, Oxford

In 1661 Wren left London to become Professor of Astronomy at Oxford. The Archbishop of Canterbury now asked Wren to design a 'Theatre' in Oxford, named the 'Sheldonian' after Sheldon, the Archbishop. This was one of Wren's first buildings, but it shows some of his best qualities. His inventiveness can be seen in the 'truss' he designed to support the very wide ceiling he required – too wide for any normal tree-trunk to span. It was made of beams which hooked into other beams lying below them, and showed the skill of a man who was later going to hoist thousands of tons of masonry over London.

The interior was not a theatre in the usual sense, but a great hall for meetings and ceremonies with a throne for the vice-chancellor of the university. But it was laid out in imitation of the ground plan of the ancient Theatre of Marcellus at Rome, which was an open-air theatre, and could be covered with tarpaulins if it ever happened to rain. Wren could hardly expect it not to rain in England, so his building was permanently roofed. But he had the amusing idea of fixing imitation ropes across the ceiling, through which you can see a painted sky, thanks to the painted cherubs who are pushing the tarpaulins back. (In the middle, by the way, is Truth, 'descending upon the Arts and Sciences'. Envy is plunging down to hideous ruin, smothered in snakes.) The whole interior has something light and fanciful about it. We can well imagine an opera by Wren's younger contemporary Purcell being performed in such a setting: it has the same buoyancy and zest as the music for *Dido and Aeneas* and *The Fairy Queen*.

Wren may have taken a hand in several other Oxford buildings. He certainly designed the elaborate tower (known as Tom Tower) crowning the Gothic entrance of Christ Church, and he also designed lodgings at Trinity College, Oxford, though only part of these remain.

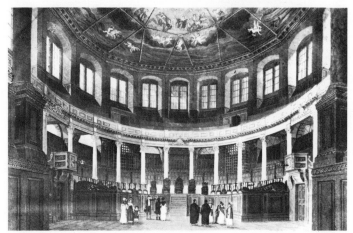

College buildings in Cambridge

Soon after 1660, Wren's uncle Matthew, the Bishop of Ely, gave money to Pembroke College, Cambridge, to build a chapel, in thanksgiving for his liberation from the Tower of London. There can be almost no doubt that Wren designed it.

There had been few classical buildings in Cambridge before the Civil War, and even these had been made without much reference to the Italian books of designs which Wren was now to use. Pembroke chapel was certainly the first college chapel to look like a classical temple, and it is particularly like one drawn by the Italian Sebastiano Serlio. It is very simple, but has pilasters and a pediment (the triangular shape crowning the pilasters) at the west end, even though one cannot enter the chapel that way, as one could enter a temple. It certainly made an impression when it was completed. Soon after, Wren was asked to design a similar building at Emmanuel College.

To understand what Wren did at Emmanuel we have to look at another chapel in Cambridge, built about thirty years earlier at Peterhouse, where his uncle Matthew had been Master. This was still a Gothic building, so far as the windows were concerned, but used some Renaissance decorations such as shell-shaped hoods, pilasters and obelisks. The chapel was joined to either side of the court in which it stands by passageways, each carried on a line of arches—an 'arcade'. In Wren's youth (the building was later altered), these arches were all alike, and rather Gothic in shape, though supported by classical columns and pilasters. The whole façade has a charm of

A drawing of the Roman temple at Tivoli made by the sixteenth-century writer on Italian architecture, Sebastiano Serlio. Books about classical architecture played an important part in spreading the ideas of the Italian Renaissance throughout Europe.

Pembroke College chapel, Cambridge. Compare this photograph of the chapel with the drawing of the temple at Tivoli.

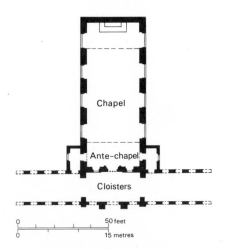

Chapel

Ante-chapel

Cloisters

0   50 feet
0   15 metres

its own, but it is a mix-up; it is not unified either in shape or in style.

In designing the Emmanuel chapel Wren made the central building and the two wings into one whole. The chapel itself is like the Pembroke one, but the buildings either side no longer stop abruptly as they reach the middle; the row of windows continues along the whole front, as does the arcade. At the same time, each unit remains distinct. There is the chapel, clearly defined by its giant columns and pilasters, and there are the two buildings like small houses to either side of it.

The whole Emmanuel design, though it is still not completely satisfying – the cupola (the domed turret above the pediment) has a floppy brim, like a Panama hat – shows a mind which enjoys making patterns that fit together, without spoiling any part for the sake of the whole. It also shows again Wren's ingenuity. The windows along the front all belong to a long gallery running across the façade, and the chapel itself lies behind the gallery, so that you cannot really see the west end, though you may think you see it there in the middle. The T-shaped arrangement, quite clear in the bird's-eye view, shows Wren's liking for geometrical shapes and designs.

There is similar cleverness in the great library at Trinity

right: *The Sansovino library, Venice, built between 1537 and 1558, to rehouse the library of St Mark's Cathedral.*

below right: *A cross-section through Trinity College library showing the library raised on pillars so that it occupies one and a half storeys of what appears from the outside to be a building of two equal storeys.*

below: *The foundations of Trinity College library, Cambridge. Building on marshy ground, Wren made the foundations more secure by inserting arches upside down.*

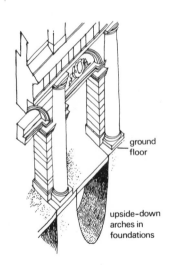

ground floor

upside-down arches in foundations

College, Cambridge, which Wren designed a few years later. Building began in 1676 (by which time he was no longer a young man). Here he thought first of creating a round building such as the great Italian Renaissance architects had favoured, but ended with a design which closes off the fourth side of a college court. It still seems to owe something to the Italians, since the idea of a library raised on an arcade already existed in the famous library of Sansovino near the waterfront in Venice. Sansovino taught Palladio, and it would be strange if Wren had not seen illustrations of the work of such a well-known architect. Besides, the practical effect of Sansovino's design was to raise the library itself well above the waters

The east side of Trinity College library. You can see that the floor of the library actually starts about two-thirds of the way up the lower columns, where space beneath the arches is filled in.

which were liable to flood Venice, and in Wren's time all the Cambridge colleges near the river, including Trinity, ran a similar risk of flooding. True, Wren's building is much simpler; the ornamentation which looks so well in richly decorated Venice would have looked too bold in Cambridge. Yet the equal division of space between the library above and the arcade below, the balustrade, the statues lining the roof, all make for a resemblance to the Venice library.

What is not so apparent is the way in which Wren has once again created a pleasing effect by illusion. The Trinity library has not in fact two equally high floors, but one deep room that occupies one and a half storeys, whose floor rests at the level of the bottom of the tympana, or semicircular spaces under the arches. The cut-away drawing shows clearly how this is done, and how as a result the bookshelves can all be stood below the sills of the windows. Light can come in from above the shelves, and the library is no longer the dark, cramped place which many medieval libraries were, but a place fit for scholars to work in. One of them, the great scientist Isaac Newton, was a Fellow of Trinity and a friend of Wren.

More important than this cleverness is the fact that Wren has made here a building of very fine proportions. On the west side, facing the river, the almost unvaried repetition is rather monotonous in comparison with Sansovino's design. Moreover, it was not correct by Renaissance standards to hide the staircase away in a brick 'tea-cannister' on that side, though in Wren's time few people would have had any occasion to go round the back and see it. But from a distance even the west side looks magnificent, with its pale yellow and pale red Ketton stone blending into a creamy white. The range of windows on the first floor is particularly good in proportions, though the grill-covered openings on the ground floor are sometimes too close together. On the east side, however, the façade is one of the best sights in Cambridge.

3   After the Great Fire

The Fire of 1666

Charles II had been on the throne for only six years when the whole centre of London (known as the City) was destroyed by fire. The Guildhall, the Royal Exchange, the Custom House and over thirteen thousand small homes went up in flames. At the same time the cathedral church of St Paul and eighty-seven parish churches were destroyed. An eye-witness said 'You would have thought for five days that it had been Doomsday.'

For Wren this disaster was a great opportunity. He was still only thirty-four years old, and, although he had already been asked to carry out urgent repairs to the old St Paul's Cathedral, he could never have expected to receive such a multitude of commissions as he now did. It is astonishing that one man was entrusted with so much. There were not only the City churches, more than fifty of them, to rebuild from the foundations, there was also St Paul's, and soon Charles II appointed Wren as his Surveyor-General, an office with hundreds of small duties. He was thus taking on far more than architects normally had done before his day—and he had no large staff to back him, nor even enough assistance to save him the trouble of looking after everyday chores. For example, the Surveyor-General had to see that people did not siphon off for their private use the water meant for the royal palace, and to estimate the cost of scaffolding for a coronation procession. The post also led to Wren being given still further commissions for extensions to royal palaces, and even for a completely new one (at Winchester, now destroyed). He later had commissions for Greenwich and Chelsea Hospitals too.

The Royal Exchange, destroyed in the Great Fire, was built in 1566 to attract trade to London and would have been thought of as the commercial centre of the City. The arcades are in the style of Italian buildings, increasingly imitated in sixteenth-century England. This etching was made in 1644 by Wenceslas Hollar, an artist from Prague who travelled around Europe drawing important or impressive buildings.

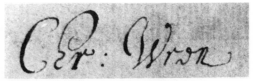

left: *The Gothic Old St Paul's was the religious centre of the City, and its proudest landmark. This drawing was made in 1656 by Hollar. Notice the repairs in Renaissance style in the western (left) part of the church.*

above: *This seventeenth-century German engraving shows the Great Fire of London as it would have appeared to an observer standing on the south bank of the River Thames in 1666.*

above right: *Charles II painted soon after his Restoration in 1660, when he was beginning to employ Wren.*

A plan for the City

Wren started off, after the Fire, in an ambitious enough way. He submitted designs to the Crown Commissioners (who were responsible for organising the rebuilding of London) for the entire replanning of London's streets. These designs never came to anything, but the plan itself, inspired by the example of Rome and an intended replanning of Paris, shows again the liveliness of his mind. Wren's new London would not have

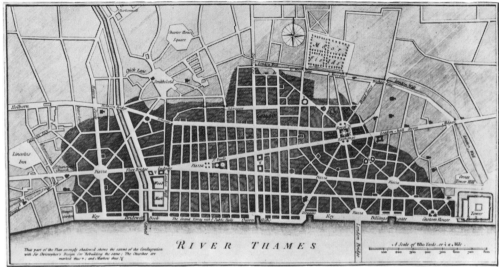

above: Wren's plan for rebuilding the city of London after the Great Fire. It was never carried out; the Londoners preferred to rebuild the old maze of streets. The shaded area shows the extent of fire damage in 1666.

been the monotonous chequerboard that was created later by neo-classical town-planners at Mannheim, for instance. Wren's London would have had several independent sets of radii, and a variety of octagons, fans, triangular or oval 'piazzas' (the Italian word for 'place' or 'square'), and embankment walks. By allowing the River Fleet to wind in something like its natural course, retaining the old main streets, and incorporating the Tower into his plan, Wren gained further variety out of the still existing features.

The Londoners had rebuilt their homes before any of this plan could be put into practice, but Wren still kept in mind the possibility of improving the appearance of the City as a whole. For this, he used both St Paul's and the new churches, whose spires and towers were for many years one of the striking features of London's skyline:

> Ships, towers, domes, theatres and temples lie
> Open unto the fields and to the sky,
> All bright and glittering in the smokeless air.

That Wordsworth, over a hundred years later, was able to write those lines, was partly due to Wren. New office blocks, together with the demolition or destruction of many of Wren's churches, have made the vision impossible today, and even St Paul's is being hidden, but there are places where something of his intention can still be enjoyed. From the south end of Waterloo Bridge you can still see St Paul's dome rising from the top of Ludgate Hill high above the houses immediately surrounding it, and St Bride's 'wedding-cake' steeple rises in tier after tier from near Fleet Street. From Upper Thames Street St Paul's can surprise you, like a liner seen over housetops in the docks. Going up Ludgate Hill, the black spire of St Martin's still acts as a pointer or marker on the way to the cathedral itself, and on the farther side, behind the east end of St Paul's, St Vedast's, Foster Lane, stands out, with its intricate play of curves, between massive white and rather boring blocks of offices. These threaten to overwhelm it, but are in fact made more interesting as foils to the church.

Wren meant all these spires to be seen, not only from the ground but from an equal height. Many of them have balconies high up, sometimes with ingenious spiral staircases. When he designed the Monument to commemorate the Great Fire he provided an even higher lookout. At one moment he even thought of making holes in the sphere crowning the Monument, out of which a man sitting inside could shoot fireworks.

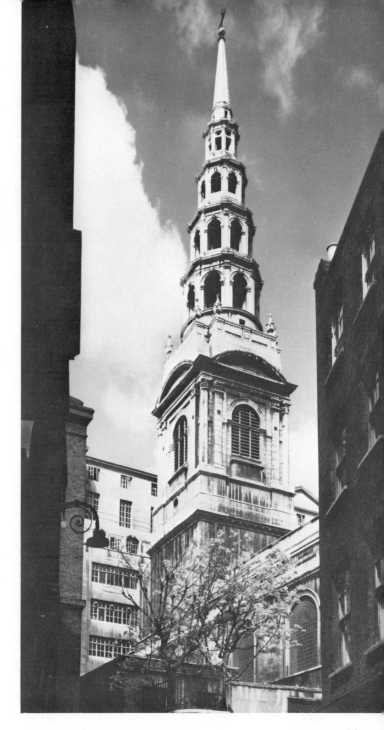

left: In 1671 Wren and Robert Hooke designed this monument – a classical column nearly 62 metres (202 ft) high – to mark the street where the Great Fire of London started.

right: The pagoda-like steeple of St Brides, Fleet Street. The diminishing size of the arches on each tier makes the steeple look higher than it really is.

The City churches

Like Wren's plan for London, the spires of the new churches are full of variety, both of shape and material. It is as though he had set out to see how many variations could be played on various themes, like Beethoven or Mozart at the piano. He had, of course, been interested in the idea of a small crowning device over a classical building, corresponding to the belfry tower of the old Gothic churches, when he placed cupolas over the two Cambridge chapels. In London, the shapes which at Cambridge had not been very inspired grew to all manner of sizes. There was usually a tower, with a first block rising to about the level of the roof of the church, then a smaller block, and above this a block with belfry openings, although even this basic pattern could be varied. Above the belfry was a pinnacle of lead or of stone, either narrowing like a long arrowhead or first containing a dome shape or a four-sided sentry-box, or a cluster of columns round a 'drum', or clusters of columns at four corners, or a series of arches, one above the other, in ever-decreasing sizes.

A STEEPLE

More than half the churches Wren built have been destroyed, either to make room for offices or shops (by far the greater number vanished for this reason) or by enemy bombing during the 1939–45 war. But the towers and steeples are so beautiful that in some cases they have been kept even though the church itself has gone.

Let us take a look at the best steeple of all, the one of St Mary-le-Bow which has the famous bells (most famous for the tradition that anyone born within hearing of these bells can claim to be a Cockney). To give them a suitable setting Wren made one of his greatest efforts.

First you notice the usual Wren tower, quite similar to several others. As you look upwards, you see that he had not

St Mary-le-Bow church, built between 1670 and 1673. The tower with its elegant steeple is not really part of the church; the plan, which was never fully realised, shows how Wren incorporated the tower in an oblong which included both the church and an arcade. The steeple is triangular in general outline, like a Gothic steeple, but built in an entirely classical style, with columns and rounded arches.

Key to plans in chapter 3

+ = *altar*
T = *tower*
↑ = *main entrance*

| 0 | | | | | 50 feet |
| 0 | | | | 15 metres |

been in grim earnest about sticking to the rules of classical architectural grammar. He may have remembered the idea of raising clusters of columns in a tower from an Italian design like the one on page 37, though some Dutch steeples may also have been in his mind. But according to the strictest authorities he should have started at the bottom with Doric and then gone on to Ionic and Corinthian, as in the Colosseum (page 6). He does start with Doric, and a kind of Ionic at the belfry level. The circle of columns round the drum, above the belfry, has capitals more like a ring of plumes than like Corinthian (though not totally unlike Corinthian), while the topmost ring of all has the same kind of plumes, with scrolls rather like the Ionic order on top of them. You will need binoculars to see this properly.

Wren knows the 'rules' but does not imagine that you have to keep to them precisely in order to create a fine building. The more we look, the more we see how he is bending the rules

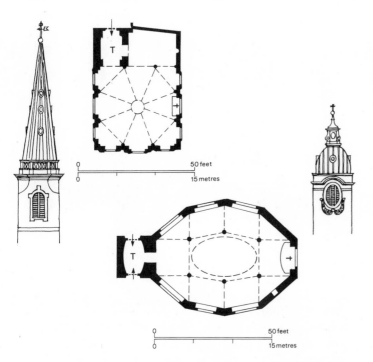

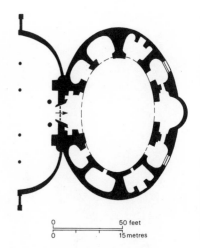

to make something very much of his own. In this he is like the French dramatist Racine, who lived at about the same time and did the same with the classical rules of tragedy.

The top of the tower of St Mary-le-Bow, as distinct from the steeple, has a cluster of curving shapes at each corner. As you see them from Cheapside, these look almost like the turrets at the corners of an English Gothic church, and that in itself shows a little of Wren's Englishness. (We shall see more soon.)

These clusters are echoed further up, first in the curves above the first drum, and then a second time in the curves above the second drum, just below the thin, almost needle-shaped spire. You can think of it, if you like, as three different notes playing in a chord or arpeggio. But just as a chord is good to hear because the notes match, so the three stages match. The belfry which forms the topmost stage of the tower, the large drum above it in the steeple, and the smaller drum higher up still have pilasters and columns of decreasing size, and all three are contained within an imaginary triangle; this must surely be one reason why the steeple is so good to see. (Don't miss the flying dragon on the top, it is part of Wren's design.)

At St Swithin (now destroyed) Wren made the steeple a pure triangle, more clearly like a Gothic steeple. At St Mary-le-Bow there is the pleasure of seeing the triangle containing so much variety. It is surprising to see the tower of St Mary's so far from the church itself. The reason for this shows well how Wren's mind worked, fitting himself to existing things rather than imposing a pattern of his own. The great Italian architect Bernini, whom Wren admired very much, and whom he once met, usually laid out a symmetrical pattern for his churches, as Wren did too, at St Benet Fink (now destroyed), for example. At St Mary-le-Bow Wren certainly meant to have symmetry: the body is almost exactly square. The old church had had the tower right alongside it, but Wren discovered that there was better soil just a little further away, on Cheapside, for the foundations of his much taller tower. So he designed a layout in which the tower was separated from the church by a corridor, and yet the whole pattern was contained in an oblong. Unfortunately, the whole was never completed as he meant it to be, but the interesting group of shapes, adapted to the soil as well as to the site, shows how willing Wren was to make the best of a situation.

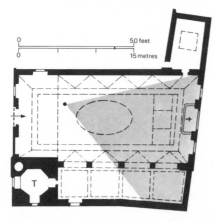

St Vedast church in the City of London. Here Wren did not create a symmetrical shape, as Bernini did (page 21), but made an irregular nave and side aisle, like a country church. The view of the interior was taken from the position indicated by the dot on the plan.

0 — 50 feet
0 — 15 metres

Few of Wren's remaining City churches were unharmed by the bombing in the Second World War. Most of the interiors you see now are restorations, sometimes entirely modern, though as much like the originals as possible. The workmanship is usually as good as it ever was, but the interiors which have mellowed with time are often more attractive. The restored interior of St Mary-le-Bow is too smooth, almost slick, in its present state. Take a look, if you are doing a 'Wren walk' round St Paul's, at St Vedast's nearby, which is practically all new. Notice how, in the plan of the church, Wren has again designed a partly traditional English building. Many old churches in England have an aisle added at one side, because the original church was too small or there was a generous benefactor. At St Vedast's Wren could have made a square or oval or round church, but has in fact made the main body a not-quite-regular oblong, with an aisle alongside which is scarcely visible until you enter it. Instead of creating a church with pure classical symmetry he has given it just a little of the feeling of familiar country churches.

It was not that Wren disagreed with the classical architects, but rather that he thought of the beauty of their buildings as 'natural', while he also admitted a different idea of what beauty is. Here are his own words:

'There are two Causes of Beauty, natural and customary. Natural is from *Geometry*, consisting in Uniformity (that is Equality) and Proportion. Customary Beauty is begotton by the Use of our Senses to those Objects which are usually pleasing to us for other Causes as Familiarity or particular Inclination breeds a Love to Things not in themselves lovely. Here lies the great Occasion of Errors; here is tried the Architect's Judgement: but always the true Test is natural or geometrical Beauty.'

below: *St Mary Abchurch. The plan, although not entirely symmetrical, is based on a circle and a square. Wren creates a feeling of space by balancing the domed roof on top of the square shape; there are no pillars to obstruct the view. You can imagine how different it feels to stand inside a church of this shape rather than in a long, Gothic, nave.*

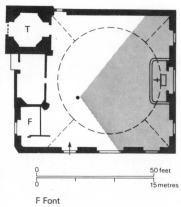

F Font

It is clear what Wren prefers. Yet he also says, very humanly, that we do often love things that are not in themselves perfectly lovely.

We see this attitude expressed in another fine interior, the one at St Mary Abchurch. Here again, Wren could have made a circular church, had he wanted to, in keeping with his own words: 'Of geometrical Figures, the Square and the Circle are most beautiful.' Instead he fitted a circular dome over the main part of the church, which is roughly square, and then allowed the space to flow out at one corner into a small rectangle containing a font, with a gallery above it. The effect is delightful, adding an intriguing nook to the spendidly spacious main body. But it is not what most Italian architects of Wren's day would have done. They would have kept to symmetry.

Circles and squares were always important for classical architects, though Wren may not have thought so for the same reasons as Leonardo (see page 5). He was certainly intending,

23

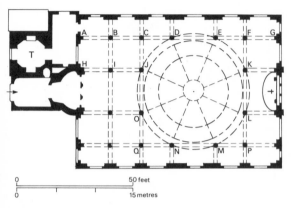

This engraving of St Stephen Walbrook, published in 1746, was dedicated to Wren's son Christopher as 'Noble Proof of his Father's Superiour Genius'. The view is drawn as if from behind the altar wall looking towards the west door. The letters on the plan are explained in the text below.

0   50 feet

0   15 metres

by now, to place a circular dome over St Paul's, and the next church we are going to look at was a kind of experiment for the cathedral.

St Stephen Walbrook, just behind the Mansion House of the Lord Mayor, is one of the best of all the City churches, partly because it has suffered less damage than many others. As you go in (and Wren wanted you to see the church from the top of the stairs, not after passing through the doors that now keep the draught out) you see columns rising on all sides in almost bewildering confusion. After your eye has taken it all in, you see that there is a circular dome supported by some of these columns. But what are all the rest for?

Looking at the plan you can see that the church has an aisle on either side. The columns and pilasters A, B, I, H make a square, and so do the columns B, C, J, I. The corresponding columns on your right are also in squares. But these aisle columns lead up to and join with other columns which make a circle, J, D, E, K, L, M, N, O, fitting into a square C, F, P, Q.

The simplest thing would have been to have a circular church, or an oval one like Bernini's on page 21. But Wren knew he would have to have aisles at St Paul's, for reasons we shall see, and this was his way of trying it out. By the way, the distance between column B and column I is almost exactly twice the distance of column B from the outside wall. Wren was using a system of mathematical proportions. But there is no need to work them out unless you are curious to know why the church has such a harmonious feeling, and to understand how the circle and the squares and triangles are related.

No words can ever match the experience of actually seeing one of Wren's City churches. The poet T. S. Eliot, who used to visit St Magnus Martyr, wrote of its 'inexplicable splendour of Ionian white and gold'. St James Garlickhythe was so full of light it was called 'Wren's lantern'. We can only leave it at that.

4 Planning the cathedral

A circular church?

We think of St Paul's today above all for its dome, yet Wren had not begun with the idea of the new cathedral having anything like it. His first design after the Fire, made in 1669–70, was more like Trinity College library, with a small dome at one end. This was opposed, however. One criticism was that it was too small. The City merchants and others wanted not only a functional cathedral, but a church which would show the importance of the capital city. Wren therefore started again, and in 1673 he hit on the grand idea to which he held for a long while. The cathedral was to be in the form of a 'Greek cross', that is a cross with equal arms. In other words it was to be like St Peter's, Rome, following Michelangelo's design. In having a dome, it was also like the Val de Grâce in Paris, which Wren saw on his one journey abroad, in 1665.

The king liked the Greek-cross plan; so did many other people. It was in fact a wonderful idea, to have curves moving inward, low down, and curves moving outward, or bulging, higher up. Your eye could sweep along the masses of stone easily, in and out, up and down, and the four arms would look the right size to support the mass of the dome. It is a simple design, easily understood as a whole. Inside, it would be perfectly symmetrical, perhaps a little monotonous, though it would have escaped the faults of Wren's final and complex design. But Wren was disappointed. There was strong opposition to this design, and he had to abandon it.

The clergy, especially the new Dean of St Paul's, Dr Stillingfleet, mostly seemed to favour a building more like the old one which was now in ruins. This had been a long, Gothic cathedral, with a tall tower and spire over the crossing (where the transepts meet the nave and chancel), though the spire had fallen down long ago. The tower marked an important place within the church, the point where ordinary people found their way barred, the point where the choir and chancel began. For the clergy, the Continental shape of Wren's new design was unwelcome for several reasons. The Church of England had broken away from the Church of Rome about a hundred and thirty years before, and the English had had to fight hard to remain separate. In 1588 the king of Spain had sent his Armada to subdue them, and they had survived that attack. King Charles II, who had returned at the Restoration, was strongly suspected of being a secret Catholic, and his brother, James Duke of York, the heir to the throne, openly admitted to having become a Catholic. No wonder, then, that some clergy suspected Charles of approving the Greek-cross design because it was like St Peter's, the church of the detested Pope in Rome.

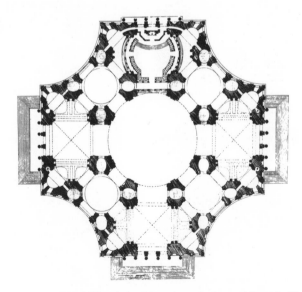

This early design of Wren's had four 'arms' of equal length, like a Greek cross. Some people wanted St Paul's to be rebuilt in Gothic style, with a long nave and short transepts, like a Latin cross.

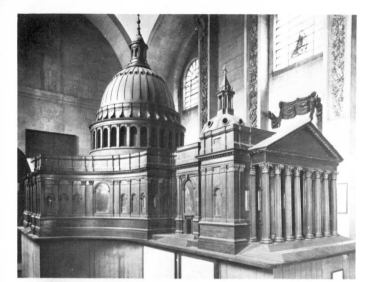

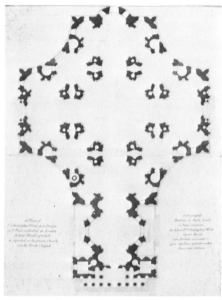

Plan of the Great Model. Here, Wren has added a short entrance to his equal-armed Greek-cross design.

suggest that the English were not so firm in their Protestantism after all, and that it did not matter to them if St Paul's did not look like its ancient companions at Canterbury and York, Lincoln, Salisbury and Exeter, for example. The Church of England, they thought, needed continuity with its own past, not a move towards the Continental Catholic style.

Wren did not see at first how much he would have to give way. The king had been so pleased with the Greek-cross idea that he ordered the so-called Great Model to be made, a fine wooden structure which can be raised on trestles so that one can stand with one's head inside the dome and see the inside from eye-level. The model is still in the Trophy Room at St Paul's. But the pressure on the king was so great that in 1674 he had to tell Wren that he must design afresh. It is said that when Wren heard the news he wept.

Dr Stillingfleet and his two colleagues who were responsible for governing the cathedral also objected that there was no longer any screen between nave and chancel. The round plan laid the choir open to the rest of the building, and did not provide for the occasions when only a few would be worshipping. But most important of all, to them, was their objection that the Church of England must be seen to be going on as it always had done. The old cathedral had been Gothic. The new one should at the very least keep to a Gothic shape. Otherwise this huge symbol in the middle of London might

The Warrant design

Wren was not too discouraged, though, and in 1675 presented another design, which met with general approval. This did what the clergy asked, and provided for a church shaped like a 'Latin cross' or crucifix. In some ways it was like the adaptation Wren had suggested even before the Fire, when the old cathedral, already altered a little by Inigo Jones in a classical way, had been in danger of falling down. Indeed it looks very much as though Wren had hastily gone back to his earlier drawings for ideas, since he provided this new design so quickly.

It is hard to see how Wren could ever have agreed to build in such a mish-mash of styles, though there were other occasions when his judgment went astray. This design, called the 'Warrant' design, since the king gave his royal warrant to it, is really a Gothic church with high nave and low aisles, tricked out with classical adornments: pilasters, domes, columns and balustrades worn like fancy dress. The tiny dome at the west end is ridiculously small in comparison with the large dome (contrast the proportions of the west towers and the dome as finally built). The large dome with its drum sits crushingly on the saucer-shaped dome beneath it. Everything suggests that Wren was leaning over backwards to provide a compromise that would be Gothic in a way and classical in a way. But it may be that he never seriously meant the Warrant design to be carried out. The king assured him that there would be no need for a second model – which would have reminded everyone of exactly what had been proposed – and that he might make alterations of an ornamental kind without obtaining approval every time.

Wren may have read more into those words than others understood them to mean. Within a short while he had begun to lay foundations which would never have suited the Warrant design, and the final form of the cathedral scarcely resembles

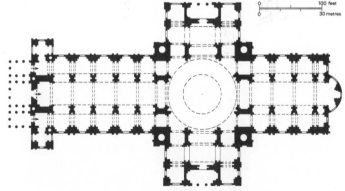

at all what had been approved. He is unlikely to have acted in this way without expecting or already having some agreement. But it is also true that for a long time to come he was still uncertain exactly how he would complete the cathedral. He must have been relieved simply to know that he could go ahead.

27

5   Building the cathedral

Demolition

The first thing to be done was to remove all that was left of the old cathedral. Where the stones had fallen down this was fairly simple, but many of the walls and columns were still standing, and they had been built to last. For a time, labourers went up the columns and hammered at the blocks of stone at their feet, to loosen them. Many men fell to their death or were crippled for life. Wren therefore invented a kind of battering-ram, which worked well, though it was sometimes two days before a column toppled under the constant battering. Then he tried gunpowder, but had to give it up when a charge was laid badly, and stones flew in all directions. No one was hurt, but some women in a nearby house were shocked when a huge block flew in through the window and thudded on the floor. It was

A seventeenth-century drawing of the ruins of the old St Paul's. On the right you can see Gothic columns and arches.

many years before all the site could be cleared, and for a time the new cathedral was rising alongside what was left of the old.

Next, there were the foundations to be thought of. Ludgate Hill, on which St Paul's stands, needed to be studied very carefully before the builders dared take the risk of piling such a colossal weight on the soil, and Wren had some tests carried out. They showed that the hill was shaped like a great sand-castle, covered with a tough but not thick crust of solidified sand. Beneath the sand was gravel, not always firm, and lower still was a kind of underground lake. Only at an even lower level did the really solid London clay begin. But since the sand and gravel had supported the old cathedral so long, Wren decided to go ahead, sinking a shaft down to the clay at one corner, where the risk was greatest. The weight was to be gigantic. Imagine the weight of one double-decker bus, eight tonnes, pressing on an area the size of this open book. That gives some idea of the pressure of the dome and its supports alone, at ground level. It was a long time before Wren felt sure that it would be safe to go ahead with the new building.

Stone for St Paul's

Getting the stone to London was a problem. Wren chose the best stone for each purpose, and the best for the outside walls came from Portland, in Dorset – a very white stone, hard enough to weather well up on the hill, with wind driving rain at it, but good to look at too. To dig it out, the quarrymen had to shovel away four and a half metres (fifteen feet) of soil and subsoil, and break up another six metres (twenty feet) of poor quality stone before they came to the best, known as the 'whit-bed'. They then had to cut a piece and haul it to the surface, where a crane loaded it on a wagon pulled by horses or mules. The wagon took the stones to a ship, which then sailed with them up the English Channel to London. Even there the job was not finished. The ships could not pass under London

The stone for St Paul's

below: *Stone is still quarried at Portland. These blocks will be used for repair work on a cathedral. In order to weather well, the stone must lie along the same plane as it did in the quarry. This is especially important when stones, such as those in the columns, support a heavy weight. The stone Wren had cut for St Paul's would have looked much the same as this.*

thedral. The whitish chalky stone quarried at Beer was also suitable for this purpose. Wren needed other good quality limestones as well, which came from the quarries at Headington, Maidstone and Burford. These were more durable and could be used for carvings on the outside of the cathedral. The limestone from Maidstone was also used for the cathedral stairs.

Most of the stone reached London by water. Sending stones by road was difficult. Such heavy weights made deep ruts, and in rainy weather wagons sank in the mud. Only the quarries at Reigate and Guildford, which were fairly near London, could do without water transport.

One stone has a special story. When Wren was considering the layout on the ground he needed a stone to mark a spot. A labourer brought one from a ruined tomb, which had on it the word 'Resurgam' – 'I shall rise again'. This was apt for the cathedral itself, and the tombstone is still preserved.

Bridge so there they transferred the load to barges, which were unloaded again at Paul's wharf. Then the stone had to be pulled up the hill through twisting, narrow streets. For very heavy blocks not only horses but capstans had to be used, dragging the stone on runners, with wedges to stop it sliding back again. Some moved only a few inches at a time.

The quarries at Caen, in northern France, Guildford and Reigate supplied soft limestone which was the best stone for the intricate carving which would decorate the inside of the ca-

Preparations on the site

Before any work began there were many more things to be done. A well had to be dug, and old tar-barrels had to be found to hold the water where it was most needed, whether for making mortar or for washing. A sawpit had to be dug. This was a hole in the ground across which you could lay a tree trunk. One man stood in the pit holding one handle of the pit-saw; another – the topsawyer – stood on level ground holding the other end, and so they worked their way down the trunk, making beams for roofs and planks for scaffolding. It was tough work, especially with oak, and more so for the man in the pit, breathing in the sawdust.

Tools had to be ordered: not only the usual ones for carpenters, but many for masons too. Some special rooms and sheds were needed. There was a place where the plans were kept, and another for nails, because these were valuable and easy to steal. There were rooms for clerks, and a room for the 'clerk of the works', John Tillison, who had to see that Wren's instructions were carried out. Tillison received £100 a year, Wren £200 a year, though for all the work he was doing, here and in other places, he may have had up to £1,000 a year.

Tools used by stone masons today. The broad chisels are for 'scappling' the stone – making it more or less ready. The narrower chisels and gouges below are for making grooves. A mason also needs steel combs and rasps for making the surface of the stone quite smooth, a mallet to use with the chisels and gouges, measures, gauges and rulers. The mitring tool is for measuring angles. The masons of St Paul's would have used tools and methods very similar to these.

30

left: *The masons of St Paul's would have signed their work with a mason's mark like this, so that the master could check each man's work.*

below left: *This modern mason is using a chisel and a mallet.*

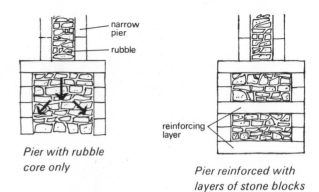

narrow pier
rubble

Pier with rubble core only

reinforcing layer

Pier reinforced with layers of stone blocks

This was worth many times as much as it would be today. A craftsman received up to £35 a year, and an unskilled labourer up to about £20.*

Wren got on well with these men, as he generally did with everyone. When the foundation stone was laid, well below ground, on 21 June 1675, he saw to it that the master mason and the master carpenter took an important part in the ceremony. He meant it to be seen how much depended on their skill. Two of the masons are today commemorated on a tablet just above Wren's own tomb.

Now the rebuilding could start. Foundations were laid for each great pier and wall, then the outline began to grow above the ground. Soon special tackle was needed for lifting the stone. For small blocks a gibbet was used, just like a gallows. For really big blocks 'sheers' were used. These were made of two tall masts joined firmly together by a beam, in the middle of which was a pulley. No man on his own could pull up these heavy blocks, so a capstan was used, like the ones sailors used for hoisting the anchor.

*A pound (£) is equal to about U.S. $2.40 in today's money.

Building the nave

After the foundations had been laid and the underground crypt built, the first storey was begun, starting at the west end. After ten years about three-quarters of this story was visible, but again there had been difficulties. The piers carrying the arches look now as though they are solid right through. But like almost all piers, they have rubble (pieces of rough stone) inside, with properly fitting blocks on the outside only. In some places it was necessary to build a narrower pier on top of a broader one underneath it in the crypt. But this narrower pier had to stand on top of the rubble, not on the outside rim of stone. As the rubble was weaker, this meant that the upper pier drove down into the lower one, and forced the surrounding stones outwards. Wren had to direct the masons that in future piers must be built with layers of stone between the rubble at regular intervals. In this way the pressure of the upper pier could be taken off the rubble.

As the walls rose, it must have been clear to some people, at any rate, that Wren was not keeping closely to the Warrant design. He had good reasons. In the building he was now planning, the dome was to be even more important than it had been before, and together with its supports it was going to weigh about 67,000 tonnes. He had to have walls and buttresses strong enough to support it, and one way of making sure of this was to thicken the walls of the aisles. Alternatively, he could make them twice as high as they really needed to be. The heavier the wall, the more pressure it would exert downwards, and the more pressure it could take sideways, from the dome. So although the aisle was not as high as the nave, the *outside* wall of the aisle was just as high as the middle of the

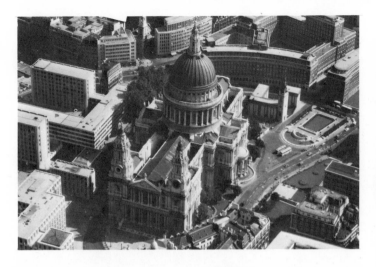

nave. You can see from the aerial photograph how this looks from above. You can also see that Wren has kept partly to the Warrant design in making a Gothic kind of church with a high nave and low aisles, but has not let this show on the outside. From the outside, the height of the walls is the same all the way round, but inside the outer screen he has built a low room over each aisle, and above this 'flying buttresses', to shore up the upper wall of the nave.

Wren shows here the cleverness he used in Cambridge to disguise what his building was like. Only Gothic buildings, not classical ones, normally had flying buttresses. Some present-day critics who believe that a building should always show outwardly what it is like inside condemn him for this conceal-ment. Yet you have only to look at that dome to see that it would not do to show only the narrow nave supporting it. The outside walls on the second storey are necessary for the impression of strength they give. The massive curves of the dome need such apparently massive areas of masonry to support them, even if the support is, in fact, supplied without so much stonework. Wren was thinking not only that the build-ing must be strong, but that it must look strong.

Gradually the arches were completed, and some people must have seen that Wren was in fact making a nave rather like that of St Peter's, Rome, after all. (A nave had been added to the basilica in Rome early in the seventeenth century, but the overall plan still incorporated the round shape which Michelangelo had developed from Bramante's design.) The

powerful and massive piers rested solidly on the ground like elephants' legs. For the stones were being built up to take the weight not only of the second storey, but also of the dome, the shape of which still had to be determined. Though the arches were not exactly triumphal arches, their giant strength still suggested the grandeur of the ancient Roman Empire.

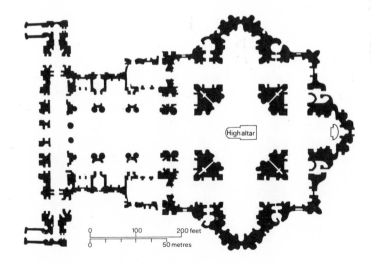

Ground plan of St Peter's, Rome, in the seventeenth century. Compare this with the final ground plan of St Paul's on page 35.

In 1684 the Thames froze several feet down and oxen were roasted on the ice. This picture was made by Abraham Hondius; the view is from St Paul's Wharf looking towards London Bridge.

Difficulties

After some years all this work came to a halt. There were still more problems, not all of them new. It was difficult to get loads to St Paul's through the crowded streets, and there was scarcely space enough round the cathedral to store all the stone and tackle as well as the paint, wood, cement, mortar and lead. The rainwater caused trouble for, although Wren made gutters, in heavy downpours the rain swept down Ludgate Hill carrying mud and debris from the building site with it, and sometimes it flooded into shops. In the end a special sewer had to be built to pacify the shopkeepers. Then the Thames froze over, and there were severe wintry conditions which not only halted supplies, but meant that the floor of the cathedral had to be constantly swept clear of snow, to prevent water getting into the foundations. The blocks sent from Portland were too often of the wrong size, despite the fact that models had been sent to show what was wanted.

Thieves went on stealing even the lead from the roof, after it had been laid. Watchmen and guard-dogs had to be stationed round the site, both against thieves and against hooligans who climbed in to smash or deface anything they could get at.

But these troubles were nothing compared with what happened after 1685 when the Catholic Duke of York became King James II. Wren's friend Sancroft, the Archbishop of Canterbury, was imprisoned in the Tower for opposing James, and Wren lost the support of several other important churchmen for similar reasons. Then he feared that the money for St Paul's would not be forthcoming. Some of this money came from private subscriptions, some from a tax on the coal brought to London from Newcastle. Wren was afraid that when Parliament came to consider this coal-tax again in 1687 they might refuse to provide for St Paul's, for they would oppose a project favoured by the king. Partly because of this, Wren got himself elected a Member of Parliament so that he could speak in his own cause.

Even when James II gave up the throne in 1688 and fled to France, the situation remained difficult. The king of France promised James his support against Mary, James' Protestant daughter, and her husband, William, who had become rulers of England at Parliament's invitation. This meant war between France and England, and it also meant that the English navy would need the best oak timber available to build new ships. But Wren needed the oak too, and he had to use his wits to get in first. Wren's problems increased when the French navy began to pursue English ships in the Channel, including the ships bringing stone for St Paul's from Portland. One of the heavily laden ships put on so much sail when it was chased by a French privateer that it capsized and sank. Four other ships were captured by the French—one of them, luckily, was sold

below: *The final ground plan of St Paul's.*

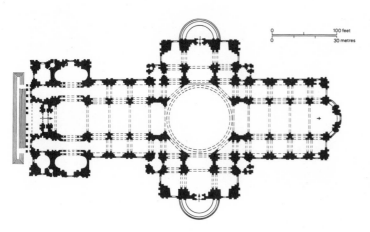

below: *This eighteenth-century view looking north-east under the dome of St Paul's shows the crossing, where the nave, chancel and transepts meet. The double 'arches' which support the dome have been made to look as much like the high arches leading to the chancel and transepts as possible.*

with its contents to the Dutch and bought back from them later. Wren also had to defend his quarrymen and sailors from being forced to join the English navy against their will. He managed to get a special regulation passed, excusing them from naval service. Another effect of the French activity was to reduce the number of ships bringing coal down the east coast from Newcastle, which in turn reduced the money for St Paul's from the coal-tax.

Building continues

After a few years of King William's reign, things improved. By 1696, over twenty years after laying the foundation stone, Wren had erected the whole of the first storey and about half of the second.

Meanwhile, it had become clear what changes Wren had made to the Warrant design (see page 27). The aerial photograph on page 33 shows that the dome rests on a square block, with two stubby transepts jutting out on two sides, north and south. The nave, although it is quite long, has been made to look shorter by widening the entrance into a portico (the three large ovals near the west end of the ground plan) and an atrium (or colonnaded entrance), and making this wider section so long that only three bays of the nave remain before the crossing is reached. So the nave and the chancel are made to look equal in length to each other, and not very much longer than

the transepts. You can see this effect from under the dome inside the cathedral: there are two transepts and two slightly longer arms. It is not a Greek cross, but it is also much less of a church with a Gothic plan than the Warrant design had been. Wren had got back as near as he could to the Great Model, his favourite design. But he had not merely been asserting his own preference for a building with equal arms. The building he was designing now simply had to do everything possible to keep the dome supported, and the Warrant design, with its narrow nave and low aisles, would not have massed stone against the sides of the central cube as well as the present design did.

All the same, this new design was a compromise, and the effect shows. At the crossing, where the nave, chancel and transepts meet, Wren had wanted to raise his dome on eight piers equally spaced out. In laying the foundations for his new design he had made the aisles narrower in relation to the nave than they had been in the Warrant design, and this led him into some slightly awkward arrangements. Four of the openings in the crossing have two arches instead of one, and the lower arch does not match the curve of the higher. Not so noticeable is the way in which the upper arch is really not a semicircular arch, as it seems to be, but is partly cut into the

far left: *A design, made in about 1650, for one of the twin bell towers (or campanili) for St Peter's, Rome, by the Italian architect Gianlorenzo Bernini. The towers were never built.*

left: *Wren's twin towers for St Paul's.*

stone pillar across which it appears to run. This was the price Wren had to pay for trying to meet the requirements of those people who had wanted a more traditional church. His original model would have been more straightforward. Still, he has managed an imposing central space, with no really damaging flaws.

It was not part of Wren's design to decorate the roof of the chancel with birds, animals and fishes. The rather gaudy mosaics were put there in the 1890s. It may be amusing to look for the hippo and elephants and comical monsters spouting water, but Wren would have disliked them very much. However, he might have accepted a few of the many other alterations made to the chancel since his day: the canopy over the altar, for instance.

THE WEST TOWERS

By 1706 the two storeys were complete from end to end. There still remained the designing of the two western towers and the dome. The towers were part of the whole western façade, which had already cost some thought. Would it be better to

have giant columns running up the whole height from the steps to the triangular pediment, or to have two sets of thinner columns placed one above the other? The giant columns would have looked extremely powerful. But, partly for practical reasons, Wren decided on the two sets of columns in pairs. This had the advantage of repeating the pairs of pilasters which run round the whole building, and so unify it. (Look at the picture of the outside on page 39.)

Having twin towers at the west end probably appealed to Wren not only because it was customary to have something similar in Norman and Gothic cathedrals, but also because Italian architects had provided them for St Peter's. The effect is like two guardians standing watch before the dome.

The question to be decided was the shape of the towers. It would have been unlike Wren to have designed anything so flame-like in outline as Bernini's proposed bell-tower for St Peter's. Wren's towers, though not unlike the twin towers at S. Agnese, Rome, by the great Italian architect Borromini, are more regular and harmonious than Borromini's. The towers of S. Agnese are oval, not round, and they are much more ornamented. Wren's are stately and majestic, but look

right: *S. Agnese in Rome, with twin bell towers designed by Francesco Borromini in 1652.*

far right: *This cross-section through the dome of St Paul's, drawn in 1755, shows the three layers of its construction.*

the same from all angles, whereas Borromini's ovals constantly offer different views. However, as you look at Wren's towers while walking round the outside of St Paul's their relationship with the lantern on top of the dome does continually change.

THE DOME

The last problem of all was the dome itself. Not only did its construction present difficulties, but the shape was an even harder problem to solve.

The simplest dome to build would be rather like a narrow ice-cream cone upside down—the weight would thrust down the sides of the cone almost vertically, and thus avoid pushing the walls of the drum outwards. But the sight of such a dome could be ridiculous, almost like a clown's hat, to modern eyes. Besides, Wren wanted to make the dome form part of the interior view; he wanted people to look up from inside at a shape a little like a half melon. Yet such a shape would push the walls of the drum outwards too strongly, and help to make the whole top collapse. How were the two ideas of the dome to be combined, so that it would look well from both inside and outside without being dangerous? He decided to make a tall cone of brick, so that this would carry most of the weight. Beneath it would be a smaller dome, which the people inside the cathedral would see. But outside would be the sturdy shape which we now know. This was to be made of great sheets of lead, nailed to timbers which in turn were fixed to the brick cone. You can see from the drawing how the three domes worked together. Much of the weight of the outer dome rested on the brick cone. The weight of this joined the weight of the inside dome and the thrust of the two went down the very slightly sloping columns of the drum and was received by the corners of the square structure beneath. These in turn were held firm by the external walls which Wren had thickened, and by his broader nave and chancel. Most of the church helped to take the strain.

Yet even now there were doubts in Wren's mind. After the church had been under construction for twenty-five years or so, cracks began to appear in some places. The ground was probably giving way under the weight, and some parts of the cathedral were sinking faster than others. Wren gave orders for the stones to be clamped together with irons, placed a metal chain round the drum to stop it from bulging, and another chain higher up. He was sorry to do so, because he always tried to work out mathematically what the strains would be. But the crust of harder soil on Ludgate Hill might be more risky than he had bargained for, and he had to make doubly sure. It has only been in this century, in fact, that concrete has had to be squeezed in under the foundations (a process called 'grouting'), and Wren could hardly have expected such a shaking as the cathedral has had from heavy modern traffic, let alone from the Underground.

While the dome was being built, Wren often had himself hoisted up in a basket to see the detail of the work. He was around seventy now, but still fit for years of work, and still thinking how to make St Paul's represent the ideal he had in mind, despite the compromises he was forced to make. He decided at length, for instance, not to have the columns on the outside of the drum, the so-called 'peristyle', in pairs, as at St Peter's, but at regular intervals, and to place a niche in every fourth space. This gives a musical effect: your eye runs along 1, 2, 3, then glides over 4 and starts on 1, 2, 3 again, and so on right the way round.

Wren arrived at the final shape of the dome only after many experiments. It is certainly the best thing about the whole cathedral. Criticisms can be made of the crossing, the windows in the side walls and the masking of the buttresses, but it is hard to see how the outside of the dome could have been bettered. It is completely steady and at rest. Where St Peter's dome leads your eye upwards all the time, St Paul's seems to sit on its peristyle with total assurance. Even the Great Model

did not have this great, settled peace. And once again Wren has placed his circle over a square.

But it is a peace in the midst of all kinds of interconnections, echoes and reflections of one part of the building in another. There is not only the echo of the lantern in the western towers; there is the echo of the whole dome in the clock face and in the curved porticoes of the north and south transepts. Also the three large triangular pediments over the west, north and south entrances are echoed in the smaller pediments on either side, and there is the unifying repetition of these smaller pedi-

ments all the way round the second storey (as well as repetition of the pairs of pilasters already mentioned). The balustrade round the top of the drum, just below the dome, corresponds with the balustrade running round the greater part of the second storey. Everywhere curves and triangles, circles and squares answer to one another and make up a symphonic whole. It would be worth while to make notes on the number of such correspondences you can spot. But there are also quite casual harmonies, like the arrangement of statues and vases on the west front. It is not all geometry and wit.

below: A wrought-iron screen near the altar by the French craftsman, Jean Tijou, who came to England to work in St Paul's from 1691 to 1709.

bottom left: Thornhill's painting on the inside of the dome of St Paul's.

opposite: The view down the nave of St Paul's Cathedral. The arches are rather like those of the church at Mantua on page 7, which resemble Roman triumphal arches.

below: Wood-carving from the choir stalls by Grinling Gibbons.

Decorations

Meanwhile, there had been the inside to decorate. For this, Wren was lucky to find some of the best craftsmen and artists who have ever worked in England. There was ironwork by the Frenchman Jean Tijou, which you can see in the tall screens close by the altar. There was wood-carving by Grinling Gibbons, who made the choir stalls, and who was so skilful that he could whittle wood down to the thickness of a blade of grass. (Outside, we should add, there was stone-carving by the Dane, Gabriel Cibber, in the transept pediments, and later on by Francis Bird, who carved the 'Conversion of St Paul' for the west pediment.) There was a fine organ and organ-case by 'Father' Schmidt, or Smith, with splendid carving, though Wren had to wait a long time for it. And there was the careful blending of stone with stone which went on every day to make the harmonious colouring which you will notice as soon as you go in, as well as plastering, carried out by men like Henry Doogood and Chrystom Wilkins. All these contribute something towards the powerful impression that the inside makes. You walk down the nave towards the central space, with the grand triumphal arches on either side. The sense of wonder as you step out under the great dome can perhaps be compared

with Handel's Hallelujah Chorus – the triumphant moment of a great oratorio. But there is a lot more in detail to be enjoyed, even after that.

In spite of all these helpers, progress was slow. There was a fire which might have threatened to bring the whole building down again. There was a landslide at the quarry, and other delays which meant Wren had to take a coach down to Portland to see for himself what was happening. And the new clergy who came to govern the cathedral in Queen Anne's reign – she succeeded William III in 1702 – seem to have thought Wren was getting too old for the job. They opposed him over many of the finishing touches, and insisted for instance on a balustrade along the top of the side walls, which Wren did not want at all. (He got snappish for once, and said 'Ladies think nothing well without an edging.') They also insisted that the inside of the dome had to be painted by Sir James Thornhill,

much against Wren's wishes. Thornhill's work does spoil the inside. It is meant to deceive the eye by making out that there are tall arches above the painted pilasters inside the peristyle, but the arches are too tall, compared with the pilasters, and do not deceive the eye – on the contrary, they look very curvy and obviously painted on. The lack of colour also makes it dull.

One old man in Wren's day was not the least impressed with any of the building:

'"Church!" replied he, "'tis no more like a church than I am. Adsheart! It's more by half like a goosepie I have seen at my landlord's, and this embroidered hole in the middle of the top is like the place in the upper-crust, where they put in the butter . . ."'

And perhaps Parliament thought the same, for in 1697 they told Wren he was making a slow job of it, and cut his pay in half till he had finished. The cathedral was officially declared finished in 1711, though the year did not see the end of his troubles, for in 1718 he was dismissed from the Surveyorship. He had reached the ripe old age of eighty-six, it is true, but after such long service he could have expected to be treated more gently. Still, he could say in the five years of his retirement that his cathedral was complete in all that mattered. The dome was built, and the 'lantern' had been hoisted to the top, with its great copper ball and cross which are 112 metres (366 feet) above ground level, and still visible, when the sun strikes them, from as far away as Hampstead Heath. He did not know that when he died his memorial would be carved with the Latin words: *Lector si monumentum requiris, circumspice* – 'Reader, if you seek a monument, look about you'. But he must have been thinking for a long time that his monument would be the cathedral. It is still his personal triumph, to this day.

6   Architecture: a new profession

You might have thought that the task of rebuilding St Paul's would have taken all Wren's time and energy during these years. But he was a very active man and never short of ideas; remember the great variety of designs he produced for the City churches and indeed for St Paul's. As Surveyor-General it was Wren's duty to design any buildings which the king commissioned. For instance the hospital for retired soldiers at Chelsea and the one for sailors at Greenwich, as well as the palace of Hampton Court, were all planned and built while work on St Paul's was still going on.

The architecture of the new Caesars

We can see Wren's work now as part of a European movement to return to the architecture of Rome. This is particularly true of his palatial buildings at Hampton Court and Greenwich, and others now destroyed. The kings who ruled right across Europe, from Louis XIV in France to Peter the Great in Russia, saw themselves as a new kind of Caesar, and their palaces showed that.

Britain was developing differently, however. After 1688 the kings of England handed over a large share of their power to Parliament, and were either unwilling or unable to build on quite the scale of the Hermitage at Petersburg (now Leningrad) or Louis' palace at Versailles. But they did a certain amount of building. William III, who came to the throne in 1688, intended to sweep away the jumble of Tudor courtyards which had been built at Hampton Court a century and a half earlier. (It was thought that a palace at that site would be good for the king's asthma.) But Parliament did not allow him nearly enough money to compete with the European despots, and so Wren's

Greenwich Hospital, seen from across the River Thames. Wren's classical details, such as domes, columns and archways, were carefully calculated to avoid an overpowering feeling, although the building is very large. He also allows a view of Inigo Jones's 'Queen's House' (1616–35) in the distance.

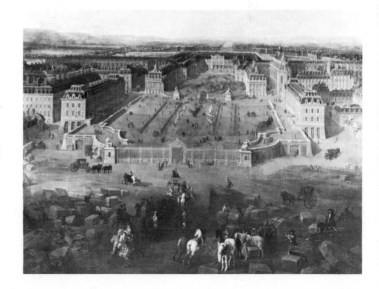

right: *Louis XIV's palace at Versailles, built between 1669 and 1685, just outside Paris. This painting was made in 1772.*

part of the palace is merely grafted onto the much larger area of buildings left by Henry VIII.

Wren's part of Hampton Court, though fairly large, is not a conscious display of royal magnificence as Versailles is, for example. The style of the building does not seek to emphasise the difference between the king and his subjects and, being largely made of a particularly good light red brick, it is a little more like a house than a palace. Yet the decorative lines of white stone (called string-courses) give it grandeur. They also help to unify each side of the building. There are features to carry your eye upwards: the tall, slender windows on the garden front, shown in the picture, point up to the round windows contrasting with square ones, which stand above them. (Once again Wren uses his two 'most beautiful' geometrical figures.) But the string-courses, running horizontally, make a balance with the upward movement. The white quoins (stone blocks in piles at the corners) help to encase the front, like a picture frame, preventing the eye from wandering beyond it.

The effect of the brickwork, which has very fine joints, allows the eye to run smoothly over the surface without hindrance from thick mortar, although each brick can be seen distinctly. The white stone centrepiece of the front acts as a focal point for the eye, but again the columns are slender like the windows. This effect is not suggestive of power and majesty as broad windows and massive columns would have been. Greenwich and Chelsea Hospitals are just as free from overpowering strength, despite the great area they cover. Wren's architecture reflects the growing feeling in England that since kings were not appointed by divine right they needed stately dignity but not the grandeur of 'The Sun-King', as Louis XIV of France was called.

Wren eclipsed

The most English quality in Wren was his willingness to compromise, not to insist on having his own way if this seemed to be against the wishes of most of the people concerned. Yet just this ability to adapt his style to what was required resulted in a good deal of criticism of him after his death in 1723. It was partly political feeling and partly fashion. The aristocracy which really ruled Britain in the eighteenth century disliked anything connected with the Stuart kings for whom Wren had begun most of his work. They also believed that architects should conform to absolute principles like those Palladio had discovered. So Wren's ingenuity in fitting his City churches into the old sites, in creating his great dome despite the complications caused by the different designs, his willingness to adapt himself to designing a Gothic-looking building if occasion demanded, and his readiness to face any problem with an open mind, all began to count against him.

Wren had important followers. Nicholas Hawksmoor, who designed some striking churches in the East End of London, and Sir John Vanbrugh, the architect of Blenheim Palace and Castle Howard, both admired him. Both these architects worked hand in hand with Wren in his old age, and although they had their own individual styles it is sometimes hard to tell how much of Wren's work after 1700 is really due to them.

The opposition to Wren was led by Lord Burlington, who built Chiswick House, London, in the late 1720s in imitation of the famous Villa Rotonda by Palladio. He also worked with William Kent in designing Holkham Hall in Norfolk. (Kent was the designer of the Horse Guards, Whitehall, facing Inigo Jones's Banqueting House.) Even James Gibbs, who designed very much in Wren's style, adapted himself to Palladianism, as can be seen in his design for the great house at Ditchley, Oxfordshire. Yet by the second half of the eighteenth century taste had changed again, and, although classical architecture was still the main fashion, the buildings of Robert Adam looked neither to Wren nor to Palladio, but to principles devised by Adam, based on his own researches in Italy.

Later still, the whole classical tradition was challenged. John Ruskin, writing in the middle of the nineteenth century, was all for Gothic, as were some other Victorians – though the truth is that architects were beginning to experiment with every conceivable style: Indian, Chinese, Egyptian, primitive, medieval and Renaissance. Ruskin went so far as to call the Greek and Roman tradition not only pagan, but morally corrupt; it was unsuited to a truly Christian country.

Such denunciation did not prevent Wren being imitated so much, in the late nineteenth century, that punsters devised a hideous though suitable word for it: 'Wrenaissance'. Most towns in England show some weak copy from this period.

But the end of classicism was in sight. By 1900 very few leading architects thought in terms of classical orders, pilasters and triumphal arches, though official buildings went on including them till after the end of the Second World War. The twentieth century has stopped looking back to Greece and Rome and is trying in hundreds of ways to meet the demand for new buildings in a rational and scientific way. Wren now seems as out of date as the Colosseum. Yet architecture has not cut off all roots in the past. There are still architects like Le Corbusier, perhaps the most famous of all in recent years, who build in a more complex relationship to the human form, but who still use the human form as a basis for their proportions. An ancient Greek wrote 'Man, the measure of all things'. That idea is still alive in some forms of modern architecture.

Later styles of architecture

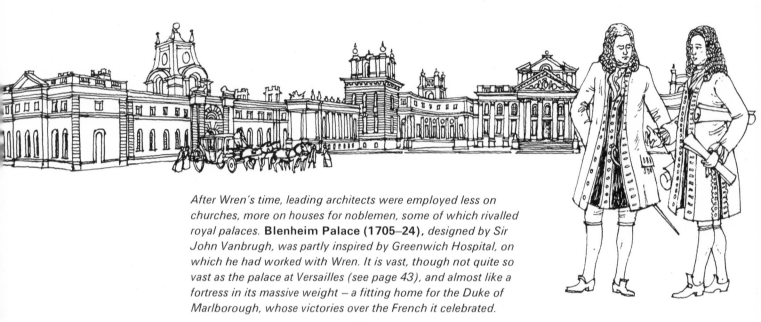

After Wren's time, leading architects were employed less on churches, more on houses for noblemen, some of which rivalled royal palaces. **Blenheim Palace (1705–24),** designed by Sir John Vanbrugh, was partly inspired by Greenwich Hospital, on which he had worked with Wren. It is vast, though not quite so vast as the palace at Versailles (see page 43), and almost like a fortress in its massive weight – a fitting home for the Duke of Marlborough, whose victories over the French it celebrated.

Lord Burlington and other architects such as Colin Campbell disapproved of Wren for departing from the principles of Palladio, first introduced by Inigo Jones. This small house at **Chiswick,** London, begun in **1725,** resembles Palladio's Villa Rotonda near Venice. It was meant not for everyday use, but for entertaining writers and artists.

Robert Adam visited Italy and returned with new ideas for classical design. He was commissioned in **1767** to make additions to the house at **Kenwood,** Hampstead Heath, London, and designed this façade to unify the additions with the existing parts, but the ornamental detail has since been much altered. The interior of the Library, the 'Adam Room', is regarded as his supreme masterpiece.

In the nineteenth century many styles came into use, a favourite being the Gothic, which had never quite died out in England, and which some felt was the true national style (though Germany and France also had 'Gothic Revivals'). **Eaton Hall,** Cheshire, largely remodelled in **1870** by Alfred Waterhouse, recalls medieval churches and palaces, but was in fact the home of the Duke of Westminster, who lived in only a small part of it.

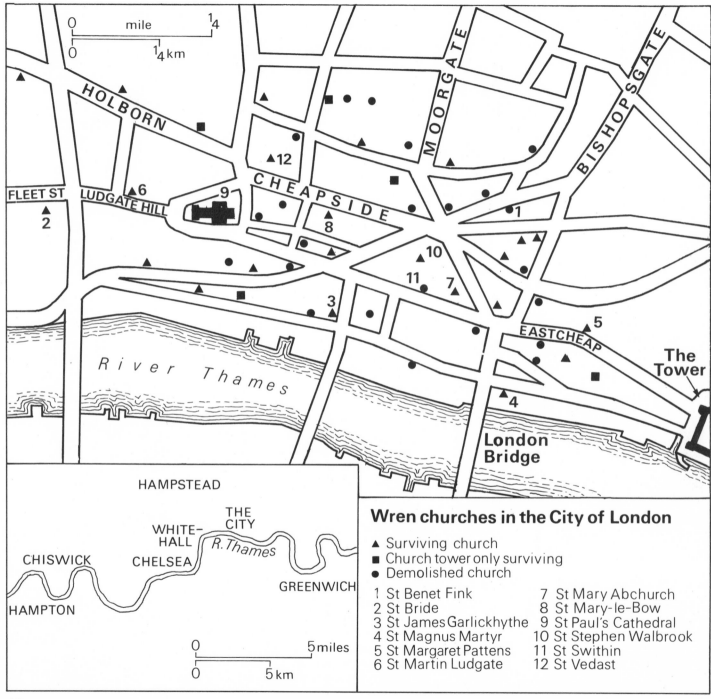

Wren churches in the City of London

▲ Surviving church
■ Church tower only surviving
● Demolished church

1 St Benet Fink	7 St Mary Abchurch
2 St Bride	8 St Mary-le-Bow
3 St James Garlickhythe	9 St Paul's Cathedral
4 St Magnus Martyr	10 St Stephen Walbrook
5 St Margaret Pattens	11 St Swithin
6 St Martin Ludgate	12 St Vedast

Glossary of Architectural Names and Terms

aisle (I'L)—a lower area on the side of a church running parallel to the nave and usually separated from it by columns

Alberti, Leon Battista—an Italian architect of the 15th century whose work played an important role in the revival of classical architecture

arcade (ar-KAID)—a series of arches supported on columns, often forming a passageway

arch—a curved structure in a building that supports the weight of the material above it

balustrade (BAL-uh-straid)—a railing supported by low columns

basilica (bah-SIL-ee-kah)—a large public building common in ancient Rome. Many early Christian churches were built in the form of basilicas.

belfry (BEL-free)—a tower in which a bell is hung

buttress—a support built against the outside wall of a building

capital—the top part of a pillar or column

chancel (CHAN-suhl)—the shorter section of a cross-shaped church, where the altar was usually located

classical orders—five styles of capitals and columns used in Roman architecture. They were known as Tuscan, Doric, Ionic, Corinthian, and Composite.

column—a vertical support usually made up of a base, a round shaft, and a capital

cupola (KEW-puh-luh)—a small tower with a dome-shaped section

dome—a large roof in the shape of a half sphere

drum—a drum-shaped section used as part of a tower or as a support for a dome

façade (fuh-SAHD)—the front of a building

flying buttress—a supporting pillar or pier connected to the outside wall of a building by an arch

gallery—a balcony

Gothic architecture—the style of architecture used during the Middle Ages. Gothic churches were tall and narrow, with pointed arches and windows of brightly colored glass

nave (NAIV)—the longer section of a cross-shaped church, extending from the entrance to the transept

Palladio, Andrea—a 16th-century Italian architect who designed many buildings in the classical style. Palladio's buildings were copied by other architects throughout Europe.

Pantheon—an ancient Roman temple used as a model for churches built during the 15th and 16th centuries

pediment (PED-uh-muhnt)—a triangular area on the front of a building below the angle formed by a sloping roof

pier (PEER)—a large pillar used to support a roof

pilaster (PIE-las-tuhr)—a pillar set against the wall of a building

portico (PORT-ee-ko)—a row of columns covered by a roof, usually at the entrance of a building

quoin (KWOIN)—an angle of a building distinguished by material different in appearance from the rest of the building

Renaissance architecture (REHN-uh-sahns)—a style of architecture based on the classical architecture of Rome, used in Europe during the 15th and 16th centuries

rubble—rough stone used to fill the interior of a pier or wall

string course—a decorative line of stone on the façade of a building

transept (TRANS-ept)—the "arm" section of a cross-shaped church

turret—a small tower

tympanum (TIM-puh-nuhm)—a semicircular space under an arch. The plural of the word is "tympana."

Vitruvius—the author of the only surviving book on Roman architecture

Index

Adam, Robert, 45, 47
Alberti (architect), 7
Anne (queen of England), 41

Banqueting House, Whitehall, 8, 9, 45
Bernini (architect), 36
Blenheim Palace, 45, 46
Borromini (architect), 36-37
Bramante (architect), 5, 7, 33
Burlington, Lord, 45, 46

Cambridge University, 12-15
Castle Howard, 45
Charles I (king of England), 8, 9
Charles II (king of England), 9, 10, 16, 25
Chelsea Hospital, 43, 44
Chiswick House, 45, 46
Christ Church College, Oxford, 11
Church of England, 9, 25
Cibber, Gabriel, 40
Civil War of 1642-6, 9, 10, 12
Colosseum, 6
Cromwell, Oliver, 9

da Vinci, Leonardo, 10, 23

Eaton Hall, 47
Emmanuel College, Cambridge, 12, 13

Gibbons, Grinling, 40
Gibbs, James, 45
Great Model of St Paul's, 26, 38-39

Greenwich Hospital, 43, 44
Gresham College, 10

Hampton Court, 43, 44
Hawksmoor, Nicholas, 45

James, Duke of York, 25, 34
James II (king of England), 34
Jones, Inigo, 8, 27, 45

Kent, William, 45
Kenwood, house at, 47

Le Corbusier (architect), 45

Marcellus, Theatre of, 11
Michelangelo, 25, 33
Middle Ages, 4, 5

Newton, Isaac, 15

orders, classical, 6
Oxford University, 10, 11

Palazzo Caprini, 7
Palladio (architect), 8, 14, 45
Pantheon, 5
Parliamentarians, 9, 10
Pembroke College chapel, Cambridge, 12, 13
Peterhouse College chapel, Cambridge, 12-13

Roman Catholic church, 9, 25
Rome, 5, 6
Royalists, 9
Ruskin, John, 45

St Benet Fink, 21
St James Garlickhythe, 24
St Magnus Martyr, 24
St Mary Abchurch, 23
St Mary-le-Bow, 19-21, 22
St Mary Major (Rome), 7
St Peter's (Rome), 5, 25, 33, 37, 38
St Stephen Walbrook, 24
St Swithin, 21
St Vedast, 22
Sansovino library, Venice, 14-15
Serlio, Sebastiano, 12
Sheldonian Theatre, Oxford, 11
Surveyor-General, Wren as, 16, 43

Thornhill, Sir James, 41-42
Tijou, Jean, 40
Trinity College, Oxford, 11; library at, 13-15, 25

Vanbrugh, Sir John, 45, 46
Versailles, palace of, 43, 44
Villa Rotunda, 45, 46
Vitruvius, 6

Warrant design of St Paul's, 27, 31, 33, 35
William III (king of England), 34, 35, 41, 43

Acknowledgments

The author and publisher would like to thank the following for permission to reproduce illustrations:

front cover reproduced by gracious permission of Her Majesty the Queen; p.3 Ashmolean Museum, Oxford; pp.5, 6 (left), 7 (top right, bottom), 14 (top), 18 (left), 37 (left) Mansell Collection; pp.6 (right), 11 (bottom right), 12 (left), 13, 14 (bottom right), 25, 27, 36 (left) photographs Cambridge University Library; p.7 (left) Oscar Savio; pp.8, 43 (top), 44 Crown Copyright – reproduced with permission of the Controller of Her Majesty's Stationery Office; p.10 Science Museum, London; p.11 (centre) Oxford County Library; pp.12 (right), 18 (right), 20, 22, 24, 40 (top left), 41, 42 Royal Commission on Historical Monuments, Crown Copyright; p.14 (bottom right), 25, 27 The Warden and Fellows of All Souls College, Oxford; pp.16, 28, Guildhall Library, City of London; pp.17 (top, bottom left), 37 (right), 39 Peter Jackson Collection; p.17 (top right) The Royal Institute of British Architects, London; p.17 (bottom right) National Portrait Gallery; pp.19, 23 Perfecta Publications Ltd; pp.26, 35, The Librarian of St Paul's Cathedral; photographs Ronald Sheridan; pp.29, 30 (bottom right), 31 (centre) Bertl Gaye; p.31 (top) Rattee and Kett; p.33 (left) Aerofilms; pp.33 (right), 36 (right), 38 photos: Warburg Institute; p.34 Museum of London; p.40 (right) St Paul's Cathedral; p.40 (bottom) Fox Photos Ltd; p.43 (bottom) Photographie Giraudon; back cover the Curators of the Sheldonian Theatre and Thomas-Photos, Oxford.

Reconstruction drawings, diagrams and maps by Laszlo Acs, Leslie Marshall and Reg Piggott.

This eighteenth-century view looking north-east under the dome of St Paul's shows the crossing, where the nave, chancel and transepts meet.

front cover: *London as seen by the Italian artist Canaletto (1697–1768), showing how St Paul's dominated the scene, while the spires of Wren's churches made a lively skyline.*

back cover: *This portrait of Wren, begun by Antonio Verrio and completed by Sir Godfrey Kneller and Sir James Thornhill, shows him holding a ground plan of St Paul's, sitting among symbols of his many other interests. He points to a globe and a view of the Sheldonian Theatre, his first work. He would have used the pair of dividers and set square on his right in architectural drawings. At his feet is an astronomical telescope and the globe on the right may well be the model of the moon that he made in 1661. Behind him is a book of architectural designs and what seems to be an easel. In the distance are the dome of St Paul's, the Monument and the steeples of several churches designed by Wren. (The carved head has not been identified.)*

The Cambridge History Library

The Cambridge Introduction to History
Written by Trevor Cairns

PEOPLE BECOME CIVILIZED

THE ROMANS AND THEIR EMPIRE

BARBARIANS, CHRISTIANS, AND MUSLIMS

THE MIDDLE AGES

EUROPE AROUND THE WORLD

EUROPE AND THE WORLD

THE BIRTH OF MODERN EUROPE

THE OLD REGIME AND THE REVOLUTION

POWER FOR THE PEOPLE

The Cambridge Topic Books
General Editor Trevor Cairns

THE AMERICAN WAR OF INDEPENDENCE

BENIN: AN AFRICAN KINDGOM AND CULTURE

THE BUDDHA

BUILDING THE MEDIEVAL CATHEDRALS

CHRISTOPHER WREN
AND ST. PAUL'S CATHEDRAL

THE EARLIEST FARMERS AND THE FIRST CITIES

EARLY CHINA AND THE WALL

THE FIRST SHIPS AROUND THE WORLD

GANDHI AND THE STRUGGLE
FOR INDIA'S INDEPENDENCE

HERNAN CORTES: CONQUISTADOR IN MEXICO

THE INDUSTRIAL REVOLUTION BEGINS

LIFE IN A FIFTEENTH-CENTURY MONASTERY

LIFE IN A MEDIEVAL VILLAGE

LIFE IN THE IRON AGE

LIFE IN THE OLD STONE AGE

MARTIN LUTHER

MEIJI JAPAN

THE MURDER OF ARCHBISHOP THOMAS

MUSLIM SPAIN

THE NAVY THAT BEAT NAPOLEON

POMPEII

THE PYRAMIDS

THE ROMAN ARMY

THE ROMAN ENGINEERS

ST. PATRICK AND IRISH CHRISTIANITY

THE VIKING SHIPS

The Cambridge History Library will be expanded in the future to include additional volumes. Lerner Publications Company is pleased to participate in making this excellent series of books available to a wide audience of readers.

Lerner Publications Company
241 First Avenue North, Minneapolis, Minnesota 55401